Dedi

*To students of the law,
never stop improving upon yourselves.*

Table of Contents

Introduction

Why Is This Book Better Than Other How-To Law School Guides?

This book is better than other how-to law school guides because it is a guide to beating the law school curve, written by law students, for law students. This book offers a variety of methods that are proven to help you perform better in law school. Do not spend hundreds of dollars on an after-LSAT program because no program can adequately prepare students for the unique obstacles each school offers. Instead, read this guide to make better grades because it is quick and provides a first-hand experience from successful students. Other books are written by authors several years removed from being a student, and this book provides a viewpoint of students who have had great success in their law school careers using techniques included in this book.

"Beating the Law School Curve" offers effective studying tips and drills on effectively taking exams and much more. Additionally, it describes what to look for when reading the casebook, illustrates how to create arguments, and identifies defenses that will gain "A's" on exams. It also offers advice on study groups, whiteboarding, multiple-choice questions, essay writing and most importantly—exam taking. This book provides a specific guide of what to do in the weeks leading up to exams. "Beating the Law School Curve" has a chapter about transferring to another law school. Also, if in a position to transfer to a higher ranked school, this chapter provides advice on transferring. A thorough explanation of the transferring process and the benefits and drawbacks of it are inside.

Why Is This Book Unique?

This book is unique because none of the authors of this book are professors. We are students dedicated to seeing other students succeed in law school. Professors typically write literature such as supplements with in-depth analysis about particular topics. They tend to interpret only from the professor's point of view, rarely attempting to think about the mindset of the student. Occasionally, the analyses and topics are not terse but instead are written in a dense manner that is certainly outside of the scope of a 1L student. The student's ability to grasp such a concept is difficult. Thus, this book is a blueprint on how to handle class and exams from a student's point of view, as opposed to the already-lawyer or professor.

Additionally, the authors of this book are just two years removed from the infamous 1L year. Our experiences from different law schools are fresh. They will speak to the 0L, the 1L, or even the transferee who is struggling to find a blueprint for beating the law school curve.

What Is The Intended Reading Time Of The Entire Book Front-To-Back?

The intended reading time is only about 3-4 days of active reading is the intended reading time of the book. A little over twenty pages per day should easily allow the reader sufficient time to complete this book. It is an easy read. It gets straight to the point to help simplify difficult concepts and techniques for 1L success. We define success as making grades that put you in the top of your class of the law school bell curve.

What Is The Last Thing To Know Before Beginning?

All law schools are not created equal. The nationwide average law school bell curve scores fall between "B" and "C" grades. Although this is not true for all law schools, it is for most. Ultimately, this book is designed to help you, the student, earn better grades through a process the authors have found to be successful.

After reading, we hope you master the process of "Beating the Law School Curve!"

Happy reading!

Preparing for Class

As a 1L, preparing for a law school class is unlike any previous classes. The demands required of law school students vastly differ the requirements of an undergraduate or master's level class. This is due largely to the way in which law school classes are conducted. Instead of the professor calling on whichever student volunteers, professors call on students at random, often with no reasoning. Being prepared for class is crucial. A student caught unprepared may suffer some embarrassment or be given a thorough reprimand in front of the entire class. To avoid being caught unprepared for class, we have provided the student with a guide to ensure successful preparation for class.

Be Familiar With The Material

There are two tasks to undertake to guarantee preparedness for class. The first task requires familiarity with the material already covered in class. Law school has concepts of legal structure which build upon each other. As the semester progresses, the professor will refer to previous topics that require the incorporation of the material into class discussion. Thus, to maintain a working knowledge of the previously covered material, it is a good idea to create flashcards and continuously update and review them often.

Assigned Readings

Doing the assigned readings in law school is important. The primary focus of being prepared for class is to do the assigned readings. There is never an excuse for not completing the assigned readings. Staying on top of the readings needs to be a priority for any law student. Do not fall behind because it is often very difficult to catch up. If you skip the material, then grab a supplement to catch up on what was missed. After realizing the importance of the readings, there may be a temptation to read ahead. As good as an idea this sounds to be, it can also be a major detriment. Reading ahead requires working memory of a vast amount of material. In the rare event that the professor scraps a future reading assignment, then valuable time is wasted.

There are two main approaches to tackling the assigned readings. Each method has pros-and-cons. Choose the method that works best for you. The first approach to completing assigned readings is to do them during the weekend. Start every week knowing that all of the assigned readings are already completed. With the reading assignments already completed for the week, material that has already been covered can be reviewed. Also, review any difficult material. Without having to focus on reading throughout the week, devote time to any assignments like concepts and outlines. The material read over the weekend will not be as fresh, though, during class. Spend time reviewing the material before class.

A second approach to take in completing reading assignments is to complete them throughout the week. By completing assigned readings during the week, there are not difficulties recalling the specific facts of each case. There will be less time spent reviewing the readings and thus more time to utilize elsewhere. Because readings are completed during the week, more weekend time can be devoted to reviewing past material or participating in weekend study groups. The downside to this approach is the time constraint.

The best method is to create an even balance with readings. For example, on Saturdays, read for Monday's classes; on Sundays read for Tuesday's classes, etc. By completing reading assignments in this manner, more time can be devoted during the week and on the weekends to studying and outlining.

Active Reading

What new law school students may not be familiar with is how to actively read in law school. The manner of reading in law school will be much different than it was in undergraduate. Undergraduate reading requires minimum effort, and the topics are not as nuanced as the law. Law school requires active reading. The casebooks are not like reading fiction. Instead, they are nuanced groupings of information by case law that logically builds off one another.

Remember, law school requires active reading. Active reading requires note-taking and highlighting *relevant* material. Do not turn the page yellow. Therefore, actively read highlight and notate the important materials in each case.

What To Look For In Case Law

Begin the case law readings with a purpose. Go into each case fact pattern to find: (1) what did each party do; (2) what was the court's decision; (3) what rule did the court apply when making its decision; (4) how did the court arrive at the outcome; and (5) what standard of scrutiny did the court use to determine the decision.

First, according to the facts, what did each party do? As a 1L, sometimes cases can become complicated if many plaintiffs are suing a defendant. Ask first, who are the plaintiffs and defendants. Second, after identifying the parties, look to the court's decision of the case. Again, as a 1L, the law may not seem so clear at first. Many opinions are written poorly. It is difficult to understand as a student, so look to the decision second. Third, determine what rules the court used to make its decision. In case law books, the opinions are greatly edited to the relevant portion necessary for the student to learn about such area of law.

However, just as we have illustrated in this book, there is a method to the madness. The opinions typically have a structure similar to the CREAC or IRAC methods. Go and look at the rules of the opinion to know what and how to write it when encountering such a problem on the exam. Fourth, look at how the court arrived at its outcome. The opinion will yield a structural process which includes the issue, rule, analysis, and conclusion of the decision. Follow the arguments and their structure to determine how the court arrives at its outcome. Lastly, fifth, review the standard of scrutiny used by the court. This is exceptionally important in constitutional law classes, as the decision is often determined by the level of scrutiny to which the court will apply.

Active Note Taking

Active notating material serves two main purposes. First, notetaking acts as a refresher on important parts already read. Secondly, it acts as a locator for an important passage in the case. So, for instance, if there is an important part of the opinion that gives support for the argument, then make sure you highlight it. This will act as an indicator and locator.

Briefing Cases

Briefing cases. Do not do it! It wastes time and energy. It is not productive at all. Creating a quick reference guide for a case is different, though. There is a multitude of canned-briefs online. In fact, some schools offer free subscriptions to sites that include canned-briefs. Canned-briefs are good for giving an overview of the case or aiding with understanding the case. A property professor may want readings or a "briefing" of the case for a certain issue, but a real estate professor may want something entirely different. However, canned-briefs do not offer the luxury of giving the material the professor expects. It is generic, broad material. If forced by professors to brief a case, it is a good idea to create a template for briefing cases. A good template will include: (1) the facts of the case; (2) how the lower court ruled (if applicable); (3) the issue of the case; (4) the rule that the court used; (5) how that court applied that rule; and (6) the outcome of the case.

Book Briefing

Book briefing is the idea of writing out thoughts in the book to use as a reference in class. To book brief, use different colors of highlighters. The yellow-highlighted material can refer to the critical facts of the case, while the green-highlight might refer to the rule the court followed, and so on. Creating a color code for highlighted material allows for quick identification of where to locate the facts, issue, rule, application, and conclusion. It is a good idea to take note of essential issues in the margins or write down potential questions for the professor in the margins. When the dreaded moment of being called on finally arrives, start with the facts of the case. The professor is not looking for the precise details of every single fact. Instead, the professor likely is checking to see if you have read the case. Give an overview of the important facts about how the facts arose in a case. After stating the facts, the professor may ask some follow up questions. Proceed to tell the class about the decision in the case and how the court ruled. There may be some back and forth Socratic with the professor, or the professor may give a hypothetical that changes a fact of the case. If so, then detail how the case may have been different had a fact been different. There is no foolproof way to prepare for being on call. If you have read the material and can coherently discuss the issues of the case, then you will do just fine. Nobody enjoys being on call in class. Therefore, book brief, so you are prepared to be called on!

A Day In Court

When preparing for a class, treat every class session as if it was a day in court. Know the arguments that both sides will make. Apply the precedent to whichever case you are on call for, then apply it properly. The professor will see that you are prepared and can piece together the material that has been taught throughout the semester. If the application is wrong, the professor will guide you towards a better application of the law. Therefore, approaching the law school classroom as if you are in court will help you improve as a student and a future lawyer.

Inside the Classroom

Surviving The Socratic Method

What is the Socratic method in law school and what does it entail? The Socratic method is the way in which professors question a student about a case pertaining to a legal rule/principle. Contrary to the beliefs of non-law school friends, professors typically do not strictly apply it. The law school climate changes overnight, and much of the advice received pre-law school is about how to survive law school, as opposed to making "A's."

How Is The Socratic Method Applied In Law School?

The main purpose of law school's use of the Socratic method is to hold students accountable for a reading assignment. Often, the Socratic method requires an explanation of the material, or to confirming understanding of it. It requires preparation before class, so you do not look like a fool because of the surrounding peer pressure. Knowing arguments beforehand and having an idea of what will be asked in class is a great way to prepare for being questioned through the Socratic method.

Why Is The Socratic Method So Daunting To New Law School Students?

Socratic method is so daunting to new law school students because it requires the student to be questioned on the spot as to their knowledge of the case. It is okay to not understand the legal reasoning at first. But not being able to articulate a case indicates the failure to read or just pure negligence. Professors will pick up on this. The most important thing to know about the Socratic method is no one cares. The only time that other students pay attention to those on the "Socratic" spotlight is when they cannot even recall basic facts of the case. Therefore, have a working knowledge of the cases to be discussed in class so that the Socratic method will not seem so daunting.

Organization

Organization is the key to surviving the Socratic method. Follow along with the professors as they go through the case. Make sure not to be caught off guard or daydreaming. Review the material in its present time, and do not try to play catch up. Actively write in the book about what you are reading. Think about potential questions the professors might ask based on the case. What type of hypotheticals could the professor come up with, that may be used on the exam – either in multiple-choice or essay? Stay ahead if you are not called. Just because you were not called on in class, does not mean you will not be the next up. So, use the time while the professor is grilling someone else, whether it be for a minute or fifteen, to prepare for the next case or upcoming subject. Do not idle. Refresh your memory. There should not be one idle moment during class. Active reading prepares you for essays or multiple-choice while in class. Therefore, be organized, so you survive the Socratic method.

What To Look For In The Readings

Three things must be identified in each case: (1) the basic facts; (2) the arguments and defenses raised by the parties; and (3) the rule and reasoning of the court. Surviving the Socratic will be based upon the ability to regurgitate the case and apply the rule and reasoning learned from each case, as stated above. Have a system for readings and the information needed from them. Go through a checklist: (1) Have you briefed cases; (2) Are they typed out or written out; (3) Have you book briefed?

Highlight the facts, holding, and rule in different colors or make notations to identify information quickly if called upon. Be wary of using canned briefs online, they may not include all the facts or may consist of information not given in the case. Professors know when students are pretending their way through a case. For example, a website of canned-briefs may include facts and rationales that the professors will not give in class. Searching for canned-outlines can be an excellent resource for seeing what to include in an outline, but canned-briefs should always be used as a backup or as a supplement to reading. So, have your book brief written in the margins of the casebook to follow along in class rather than catching up to where the professor is. Also, this is an imperative part that is taken for granted by many new law students: make sure everything needed for class is prepared and ready to go. This is essential to be organized. It is imperative to not scramble before class. Pack it all up the night before, and take it seriously, as if making a presentation for a job. At times, the material may have been read a few days before, so be sure and refresh your memory on the subject. Finally, refresh what you already read before going to class.

First And Last Ten Minutes In Class

The first and last ten minutes in class are critical. A typical class begins with a brief overlay of the day, maybe 1-3 minutes. After that, most professors get right into their lesson. Every professor has a lesson plan, but it often runs aground after the first ten minutes due to other student's questions. Thirty minutes into an hour-and-a-half class, the attention span of students with laptops in front of them will fall drastically. Also, your colleagues could ask questions that can take the lesson plan far off track. The professors know what they want to cover, but they do not know how the class will collectively get to the points. Just like in any speech, the speaker knows what material needs to be covered, but cannot always guess the precise amount of time the speech will last.

Professors start off strong in the first 10 minutes, hitting the big points. Due to interruption and extensive class participation, the professor's lesson plan may get off track. When time begins to run out, a professor usually takes the last 10 minutes to drive home the lesson plan. So, then what should be looked for in those first and last ten minutes and why is that time critical for professor information? It is critical to pay attention during those first ten minutes because the professor is on point. The professor is delivering unadulterated information, meaning that other students haven't yet muddied the waters with irrelevant or relevant questions. Because the professor's points are unadulterated, the professor feeds the class information which will be critical to the exam during those first ten minutes. During the last ten minutes, a professor may be attempting to salvage a day's lesson if it were derailed. During this time, the professor will review the important information for the day and drive home the big points. Paying close attention during this time is imperative.

Lessons Go Off The Tracks

When the lesson goes off the tracks, be sure you make use of that time! The are several productive ways to tackle what may seem like downtime in class. No one likes being caught unprepared for a case, so reviewing an upcoming case is a good idea. Follow along with the professor and the class. As the professor asks the students questions, answer them to yourself. It is also a good idea to have something planned to do during this wasted time until the professor gets back on topic. Look at your other classes, and see which outlines need work. Check on subjects that need improvement. Also, make use of the multiple-choice practice during this time.

A quick, way of gathering knowledge, as mentioned earlier is through practice drills. Drills are also a good way of making the downtime useful because they can be done individually without context. If research is needed on another topic, then do it while the lesson plan is off the tracks. Also, this can be the useful time to update outlines. The outline segment will be discussed later, but for now, know that it is good to make use of the downtime fixing and polishing an outline.

Paying Attention To The Important Stuff

Pay attention to questions other students are asking. The chances are, you may have the same question. And the professors frequently offer helpful tips for mastering the material or clarification. Also, write down the questions the teachers are asking in class. They are asking these question for a reason, this material will likely be on the test, so take notes accordingly.

When The Professor Highlights And Repeats Cases

As the semester progresses, professors will refer back to particular cases. Professors do not usually return to cases that were already discussed, but if certain cases continuously work their way into the lesson, it is likely that this topic will be seen on the exam. Take special note of what cases the professor likes to reference and grasp the material that the professor is trying to pull from those cases.

Avoid Distractions

Some professors ban the use of laptops in class. This is done to encourage students to get involved and to prevent unnecessary distractions during class. You cannot control this. If the professor says no laptops, then no laptops. However, if given the opportunity to use laptop, then certainly take advantage and use it. Do not go surfing, do not text, others are watching, this may be distracting to them. If tempted to text or surf, then hand write notes. Distractions cannot be afforded in class. Think of every class as a $200 check being written to the school. Want to pay attention now? Do not write everything the professor says, listen, and write down the relevant, useful information. Many times, students will be so busy copying irrelevant information that they miss important aspects of the lecture.

Effective note taking requires attentiveness and knowing what to take notes on and what to ignore. You are in law school to be a lawyer, not a court reporter. Only type what you would likely write in an essay on the subject. Organize these notes. Do not blindly write everything in bullets, or line by line. Organizing notes present the ability to navigate through notes when compiling an outline more easily. Review any notes after class. Make sure you understand what was written and clean them up. Sometimes in the heat of the moment, notes can become incoherent. Fix them immediately while the material is fresh. Write down questions you have during class as the professor is talking. It is very difficult to remember all of these questions once the class is over, so promptly act if there is any uncertainty. Write it down.

Where To Sit And Sitting With The Right People

Avoid the front and back rows, as professors likely target those areas. Do not sit around students known to be disruptive (you know who they are). Idle chatter or students that can be disruptive or take up more than their fair share of desk space can be a nuisance. Be comfortable in class. Stay away from disruptors to add to attentiveness in class.

Getting To Class Early And Staying Late

Arrive to class with enough time to get situated, be ready to go, focused, and with the mind turned on. Be ready once the professor starts. Professors know who is ready and who is not. Continuously arriving late, or just getting situated when the professor is starting is a surefire way to become a target. Stay after class; do not join the rush to leave the classroom. Go through your notes to see if anything was missed, do not be afraid to approach the professor after class if any additional clarification is needed on the material that was covered for the day. Other students may have questions, listen to their questions. The answers given by the professor may be valuable information.

Participation

Participation is the bane of many law students. Since law school professors are likely to call on students at random, some are fearful to get caught off guard or unprepared. Many students can struggle to get out the right words in front of a class of fifty or more students. And yet, others are fearful that they may seem foolish in front of their classmates. Do not worry about being embarrassed. Arrive to class prepared to discuss the material.

The number one reason to participate is that some professors may give bonus points for participation. Usually, a third of letter grade is typical (e.g., B+ to A-). Be wary though; you do not want to be "that guy" who talk too much without logical reason or consideration. Professors who award grade-bumps for participation make little check marks on their attendance sheets. If after a participation grade-bump, take note of how often professors make check marks when others participate and strive to offer just as much as the leading student in the class.

Class participation also allows for engagement in the material with the professor. Through the professor's questioning, students learn to be quick on their feet with responses and will be better able to analyze arguments when it comes to exam time. Engaging in the back-and-forth with the professor allows time to see where your reasoning is right or wrong. Take note of what conclusions the professor pushes students to come to, and utilize that reasoning in your essay.

Nobody likes being put on the spot, especially for a lengthy case that may require the student to discuss in detail the issues of that case. Voluntarily participating throughout class sessions is a good way to ensure that you will not be made to participate in class involuntarily. Professors tend to target those who have not spoken, so speak up on topics you know.

Why You Should Not Participate

Yes, you read it correctly—should not participate. You should be writing instead. Outside of stating the facts, the professor is asking analytical questions. The answer is important to write down, not speak up about because they are likely to appear in some manner on the exam. For some classes, participation is a losing battle.

However, there is strategic participation as a remedy. Strategic participation is knowing when to participate and how to participate. It depends largely on the manner in which the professors call on students, but it can prove effective. How does the professor call on students? Is it randomly, alphabetically, by rows, by sections? Most professors randomly choose students, if in the other category, better luck next professor. If randomly, you are in luck. Participating in easier, softball questions, or for cases in which you are well versed or find interesting or easy to grasp, jump at the chance to participate.

No one likes being caught off guard and forced to discuss a topic they do not want to discuss. So, participate when there is enough time left in class. Make a meaningful contribution.

Outside the Classroom

Most law school time is spent outside the classroom. In this chapter, we will discuss how best to utilize your time in the minutes before a class begins, what to do as soon as class ends, and time spent outside of the classroom.

During a law school career, very little time is spent in the classroom. The majority of time during law school will be spent outside the classroom. Thus, it is crucial to utilize time outside of class efficiently. Before any class begins, be prepared for class. Before any class use the "B.E.D." technique, bathroom, eat, drink. If you have to use the bathroom or eat or drink anything during class, you may be too distracted to focus on what material is being covered in class. Additionally, if you have to step out of class to use the bathroom or quickly eat a snack, valuable class time may be missed. Always plan to arrive at each class early, with enough time to use the restroom and eat or drink anything. Also, arrive early enough to give ample time to set up the materials needed for class when the professor starts.

As soon as class ends, use the "A.R.M." technique. Ask, review, memorialize. Ask the professor any questions that come to mind during class that the professor did not get around to answering. Review any important materials that were covered in class and memorialize them. Since the majority of studying will be done outside of the classroom, it is paramount to utilize time effectively and efficiently. When not reading for class or working on outlines, devote as much time as you can to actively studying the materials the professor has covered in the classroom. There are several approaches possible to take studying outside of class. In this chapter, we will detail the methods the authors have found to be extremely helpful.

Study Groups

Taking on law school alone can be extremely difficult. It is important to surround yourself with other students who are equally committed to success. Whether you think you need a study group or not, you need one. Law school is demanding, and often, you will need to discuss topics and have a group to lean on for support. If you miss a class for any reason, those in a study group can help fill in the gaps for notes. A study group can be instrumental in getting outlines together. Create games, study with flashcards, or develop methods that the group finds helpful for studying the material.

Forming The Group

Forming the right kind of study group relieves some of the burdens of law school. However, if there are too many students in a study group, then only a few will emerge to help shoulder the burden; too few and there will not be enough students to shoulder the burdens of law school. A good study group is comprised of three to five students. A group consisting of too many students becomes a social group rather than a study group. If there are not enough students in a study group, then there may not be enough people to rely on for missed notes, outlines, or any additional needs that arise.

Once a reliable study group is formed, the group will need to determine how often group members will meet. There is no specific length of time that a successful study group meets for throughout the week. Instead, a study group should meet only as often as necessary. Some groups can maintain a fantastic working dynamic where group members can read or study side by side diligently, whereas other study groups should only meet sparingly to avoid distraction.

Throughout the semester a study group can be utilized to review assigned readings, creating flashcards or flowcharts, and filling in missed notes. It may also be helpful to use a study group as a discussion group to talk through materials covered in class. Comprehension of the subject will increase by doing this. Therefore, utilize the study group throughout the semester with the main intent to prepare for the final.

Studying For The Final Exam With Your Group

Once a study group is ready to begin preparation for the final exam, there are several ways in which the group can be utilized. Study groups often assign each member a particular class to outline. For example, if one member is tasked with developing the outline for Torts class, use the Torts notes of each of the fellow study group members. By only creating one or two outlines, time for studying will be enhanced. A major caveat to this is that each group member working on an outline must be in the same class. For instance, if in Professor Smith's Torts class, and the rest of the group members are in Professor Green's Torts class, then an outline created for the same subject may not be helpful across different professors.

As the final exam approaches, a study group can be utilized as graders for practice essays. Find a practice essay, particularly one written by the professor, and have each group member write an essay answer under timed conditions. Identify the most difficult areas that can be improved by utilizing study group members as graders of a practice essay.

If you decide to forego a study group altogether, an outlet to bounce information off of and get feedback from will still be needed. As a 1L, approach a 2L or 3L for guidance on a particular class. Professors are also great sources of information. Many professors are willing to grade practice essays, or at the very least review a practice essay with their students. Everything considered, it is difficult to go through law school without a good study group. You may be hesitant to share your notes with others or believe that you are the one student in every class who gets it. Maybe you are. Law school is an adversarial environment, but if you work together with a few students, you will achieve more and do better because of the feedback if it is intelligible.

Supplements

The use of supplements is a must. Supplements are an aid for difficult topics. If the professor does not explain the information in a cogent, coherent way, then there is no choice but to look outside the classroom for support. Supplements are that support. Achieve the edge and start supplementing. If professors tell students that supplements are not necessary, they are wrong! Not all casebooks present the material in a manner that is easy to understand. And not all professors can explain material in a way that is understood by the entire class.

As a word of caution: supplements should never be used to replace assigned readings. Instead, use them to add clarification to what has been or will be taught. Not all supplements are created equal, and not all supplements present the material in the same manner. When choosing supplements, select a supplement that adequately explains the material the professor presented in class. Most importantly, choose a supplement that presents the material in a way that is easy to grasp.

Alternative Methods

Another important tool which can be used outside the classroom is flashcards. Flashcards are important because of how simple they are to create and how versatile they can be. Buy notecards and create flashcards that can be taken anywhere. Or create notecards on an app or website and have them saved to your cell phone. Either way, flashcards are useful because they allow students to have study materials without having to carry around a hefty book or supplement. Furthermore, significant research has demonstrated how the use of flashcards can help with memorization of material.

Thankfully, the material to create flashcards is already provided by the professor. Many professors who teach their class via slides make those slides available to their students. Utilize flashcards by creating questions using information from the professor's slides. Materials that professors incorporate into their slides are the same materials that professors expect to see on in an exam answer. Thus, make flashcards that resemble a skeleton exam (more on this later); experience has taught us that top grades can be achieved when utilizing the M.A.D. method, memorize, ascertain, dissertate. By memorizing keywords, phrases, and definitions, your exam can and will stand out amongst the rest! Remember, professors grade hundreds of exams in a short amount of time. Professors who do not read every single exam in its entirety may look for key phrases or terms when awarding points. Therefore, use the <u>exact phrases</u> memorized from the flashcards to aid the professor grading exams. Help the professor give you the points needed to "<u>Beat the Law School Curve</u>."

Outlining

Without a doubt, anyone going into law school has heard about the importance of outlining. Outlines are crucial to law school success, and it is vital that you have an outline tailored to your learning style. So, what is an outline? An outline is an entire course reduced to a manageable number of pages in your own words. An outline does not need to be neat or well written; it only needs to be constructed in a manner that helps you memorize the material.

No 1L experience would be complete without the adventure of tracking down the outlines used by other students who were successful in the course, coming across a bank of outlines maintained by an organization, or finding a "good" outline online. Although outlines that you do not create yourself can be helpful, we caution anyone using an outline that was not created by the student. Outlining is a process. As you create an outline, you are creating a document that is tailored to your learning style and the way in which the professor presented material.

How Do You Begin Outlining?

How should you comprise the outline? How do you know what information should be included and excluded? Does the outline need to list every single case discussed throughout the semester? Should the outline be comprised of information that other students in the class have gotten? As with many questions in law school, the answer is: It depends. This chapter will address all of the above questions and give guidance on how to formulate an outline that is sure to keep you ahead of the curve.

Beginning An Outline

There is no doubt you will be overwhelmed with the material in your first year. A good starting point to any outline begins with identifying the topics that the professor has presented or will present. Follow the Table of Contents in your casebook and use those headings as a starting point to divide your outline into topics. If the professor skips from chapter to chapter or section to section, follow the order in which the professor presents the material.

You do not need to begin outlining after your first class. In fact, you do not need to outline for the first couple of weeks of each semester. For some students, there is a big desire to form a study group right away and begin outlining. However, you do have a few weeks to feel out the other students in your class before you begin a group outline if that is how you want to approach outlining. There is no rush to begin outlining early on in the semester. Some students may jump at the first opportunity to create a study group and begin outlining; do not do this. Instead, wait and choose a more cohesive group over a group of random students at the beginning of the semester.

After you have laid out the major topics of your outline, begin filling in the outline with material relevant to that topic. The majority of an outline should focus on three things: (1) the rules learned from each case covered; (2) the elements to those rules; and (3) exceptions to those rules. It may not be necessary to remember every single case name, often just knowing the rules and their exceptions is enough.

Gathering Materials

Gathering the materials that you need for each portion of your outline can be acquired from your casebook, class notes, and anything else that the professor has handed out in class. Usually, if the professor has handed out anything in class, it's a good idea to review this material carefully and integrate it into the outline. Be wary of adding information to an outline that was attained from outside sources. If you are missing something from your outline that you cannot find in your casebook or notes the best thing to do is to ask the professor. If meeting with the professor is not feasible, then ask a fellow student or study group member.

As you incorporate more and more material into an outline, you will begin to realize that the outline is starting to resemble a book instead of an outline. That's okay! In fact, some professors highly recommend this. According to those professors, an outline at the end of the semester should be 100 pages. These professors urge students to create large outlines, read through them and continuously reduce the material. 100 pages will quickly become sixty pages, sixty pages will become forty pages, and eventually, the outline will be twenty pages. A twenty page is much more manageable than a 100-page outline, and the twenty-page outline can be studied and read several times a day as you prepare for the final.

Cutting Material

So how do you know what material to drop and what material to keep? What to keep or discard in an outline depends highly on what the professor expects the students to know for the exam. Although we cannot predict what a particular professor will expect their students to know, we can tell you what every outline needs to include and what you can exclude. An outline should be constructed in the order in which material was taught, and it should be organized in a manner that is easy to understand. Most importantly, every outline must include the elements for every claim and defense that has been taught.

It helps to organize an outline in a manner that displays which defenses can be brought for each claim. Any exceptions or essential notes that you have regarding a claim or defense should also be included in that section of the outline. It is not necessary to include the case names and holdings of each case covered throughout the semester. Generally, there are a few key cases to include in your outline. If the professor has covered a particular case in great detail, or if that professor has referred to particular cases throughout the semester it is a good idea to include that case in your outline.

As you gradually add to your outline or when you complete your outline, you will realize that you have included lots of material that you may not need, that is okay. In reviewing a section of your outline or the entire outline, you will quickly realize that some of the material is not as important as you once thought that it was or you will already have committed that material to memory. Deciding what to do with material that you may not need or have already memorized depends significantly on how your final exam is conducted. If the professor does not allow the use of outlines for the final exam, it is a good idea to reduce your outline to include only topics that you have not committed to memory. If, however, you are allowed to use your outline during the final exam it may be worthwhile to include information that you may not necessarily need so that you can utilize that information if it is needed.

There are two significant caveats to having your outline with you in the final exam. First, having the outline with you is no excuse to put off studying that outline before the exam. The outline is more of a security blanket than an actual tool for the exam. Secondly, if you do choose to use your outline for the exam, it needs to be very well structured. Exams are given under time constraints and although it may only take a few moments to locate what you need in the exam, all those moments spent rifling through your outline will waste precious time.

When To Begin Outlining

Now that you know the basics of proper outlining procedures, you are probably wondering when you should begin outlining. Many students wait until Thanksgiving break or spring break to begin outlining, and others may have started as early as the second week of the semester. Although there is no set time of when to complete the outline, here are our recommendations. If you decide to outline with a study group, you can afford to put off outlining for a substantial amount of time because each person in a study group will have a particular assignment. It is rare that a study group would require each member to compose an outline for each class and then compile their outlines together. Instead, group outlining is most efficiently done when there is a set date on which all of the outlines need to be complete so that each group member can review the other outlines and make additions or deletions as necessary. If you decide to be a lone ranger and do all of your outlining yourself, then begin early. It is very challenging to create good outlines for all of your classes when you are just a few weeks away from the final exam. If you decide to go about outlining on your own, the recommended approach is to start outlining after the second or third week of the semester.

Often, there will not be enough material to outline after the first week. When you do an outline, be consistent, set aside an afternoon or a part of the weekend to compile the material you have from each class into your outlines. Try to stay as up to date with your outlines. Outlining can be a major chore, but if you fall weeks behind in outlining for all of your classes, it can be challenging and time-consuming to catch up.

No two students study the same or remember material in the same manner. It is essential that you discover early on the best method for you to remember the materials that the professor has taught. The importance of outlining is harped on so much because it has proven itself to be an effective way to study material. One of the best approaches to outlining is to not look at outlining as a process of making a study guide for your final exam. Look at outlining as a method of studying. As you piece together the materials for your outline, you will be working with material that will be on the exam. Take the time then to refresh your memory with those materials and attempt to commit those materials to memory as you proceed in completing the outline that you need. Therefore, work hard on creating your outline early and often to reap the benefits come exam time.

Exam Preparation

When Should I Exam Prep?

Actively begin exam prepping during the weekends throughout the school year. Do not wait until the final weeks to prepare for exams. Commit yourself to law school and treat it as a job. Work on the weekends. Perhaps the three most important days during your law school semester are Friday, Saturday, and Sunday. If you want to beat the law school curve and the rest of your classmates, then you have to outwork them consistently. This is achieved by connecting theoretical concepts early in the semester, with practical application.

Where Do I Begin?

Use the first couple of weekends during the semester and do basic google searches to look up old exams to practice exam taking. Once you go through a few exams, you will begin to see what type of questions have been repetitively asked by professors. These are likely similar questions your professor is going to test on. For example, learning the commerce clause or substantive due process clause analysis early in the semester would be extremely helpful in a constitutional law exam. To master the exam and make an "A," you must fully commit yourself to hard work and dedication on the essay portion. Daily discipline is the key to success.

Form A Study Schedule

Plan out a study schedule that is proportional to your classes. Often, because of the way law school exams are structured, the last few exams are neglected the proper preparation because a significant amount of study has gone into the first few exams. The way to combat this neglect is to distribute your time proportionally among exams.

There are a few things to consider when mapping out your study plan for finals. First, determine which exams have multiple-choice and which ones have essays. Generally, preparing for multiple-choice comes in one of two forms: (1) preparing through your professor's old course reserves or (2) preparing through a generic guide or supplement book. As to the latter, an excellent study source is always finding a multi-state bar exam book with bar formatted questions. Second, not all exams or professors are created equally. Some exams will be immensely tougher than others. So again, it is advantageous to layout your study schedule accordingly. Third, start with a division of hours per exam per day. For example, you may want to allow more time for later exams early on so that you can lay the foundation you will need after you have taken your first exam. Also, divide up the exams into first-week and second-week categories. This way, the second-week-finals exams are not neglected, and you have a set approach to take in studying for it. Now you are ready to create your actual study schedule after you have determined which of your exams you believe will consume the most substantial amount of preparation time.

Take Your Professor's Old Exams and Look at Course Reserves

Now that your study schedule is formed, you can focus on specifics. This begins with gathering any material you can find through google searches, course reserves, and the like on particular professors. For example, professors may have old multiple-choice exams in the course reserves. Being aware of how a professor asks questions will aid you in the final. In another example, be aware of current issues because they do appear with some frequency on final exams. By being familiar with a particular current issue, I evaded reading at least ten to fifteen minutes of factual background on the exam, which allowed me to begin issue-spotting and writing.

The repetitive point here is: know the professor! If you know that your professor stores course reserves, then use them to practice exam taking. Knowing how the professor will write their exam is crucial to being able to identify the issue, the level of difficulty of the question, and ultimately, get you an excellent grade on the essay or multiple-choice. These principles do not just apply to the essay, but also especially to multiple-choice questions.

Identify how your professor writes their exams, and begin studying it utilizing the following analysis: First, start with whatever information is given. If course reserves hold multiple-choice questions, then study those and look for things like the call of the question or key phrases the professor uses. Next, study the answers. Sure, it is not likely you will get some of the same questions, but we have seen it happen in exams before. Next, look at how the essay and multiple-choice questions are structured. Does it follow a pattern you learned in class? Is the question a replica of a fact-pattern from the casebook? If so, make a note of that. And study other similar questions to gain an edge on the competition. If the question is strictly an essay question, (i.e., commerce clause question), then is it something your professor consistently spoke about in class? If yes, make a note of the cases that might be associated with that particular question. Draw the analysis that you have from your in-class notes, then start applying (commerce clause) it to the question.

Talk to Upperclassmen

Often, professors use similarly structured exams. For example, in my case, the professors I had in my 1L year used the similar exam for the new 1L's that came in after me. For this reason, it is good to know upperclassmen. It is vital to address the benefits of upperclassmen within the context of exam prep here. So how or where do you find upperclassmen that can aid you in obtaining or finding the material you need for a professor's exam? Look into extracurricular activities like law review, trial team, or moot court to meet upperclassmen. What type of extracurricular activities? Being on a board, whether it be student body, law review, or a journal. Meeting upperclassmen to find exams given by the same professor the year prior is crucial. Therefore, talk to the upperclassmen.

Know Your Big Issues

Where can you scoop up points that others miss to make top grades in class? Listen to your professor while in class or look deeply into their slides. Professors speak specifically in class about precisely what they will test you on. Each time a "hint" is thrown out by a professor by harping on the same issue or set of cases when discussing an issue, it is likely that issue will be tested on the final. Take a note. Look for the big items.

Exam Preparation Tools

Now you have ideally found critical issues. Next, begin exam preparation. There are many places to start. We are going to list just a few useful tools of study for learning, applying, and regurgitating. Below is a list of tools you can use for exam preparation.

Memorization

Memorizing is the essential preparation tool for scoring A's on your exam. More so, in addition to the elements and black letter law that will guide your rules, memorization through the use of flash cards is an invaluable tool. The only obstacle you should have on exam day is reading a new fact pattern and then applying the material you have memorized. The next logical step is to memorize the information.

Mnemonics

A mnemonic is a tool to be used in law school for grouping cases and terms. For example, in a Civil Procedure class, cases like *International Shoe, Daimler AG* and *Asahi (IS, DA, A)* were all citing necessities in the exam. Each case represented an idea, rule, or both. So, to remember them, along with a large number of other cases (about fifteen in all), we created a sizeable mnemonic checklist. After each

idea or rule was extracted from a letter, we then
checked it off the list. The use of mnemonics aided
our memories in which cases we had to cite to write
the perfect essay. Additionally, mnemonics can also
be used for grouping elements. For example, in a
Contracts class, many students used the mnemonic
T-A-C-O, or Terms, Acceptance, Consideration, and
Offer, as the requirements of a valid contract. How
should I use the mnemonic technique of
memorizing? Here are a couple of examples:

- TACO (terms, acceptance, consideration,
  offer);
- QTPPPS (quantity, time, parties, place, price,
  subject matter);
- OCEAN (open, continuous, exclusive, actual,
  notorious).

Use mnemonics by memorizing the first letter of
words in an analysis, better known as the skeleton
for the exam (more on this next). For example, if you
have a Civil Procedure exam and need to remember
which cases correlate with legal rules corresponding
to diversity analysis, then you might write out
something like MGHD to remember that *Mas v.*

Perry, Gordon v. Steele, Hertz Corp v. Friend, and Diefenthal v. C.A.B. all deal with the issue of complete diversity and meeting the amount in controversy. Use the mnemonic at the very beginning of the exam when it is fresh on your mind. In a lengthy final exam, it is imperative to lay out legal rules as soon as the exam begins because the brain becomes fatigued during the later stages of the exam. If there is a mnemonic written on paper at the beginning of the test, then that will automatically trigger cases that hold legal rules to finish the long exam strong and stay on point. Once the test begins, write out your mnemonics that contain all the cases you will need. Regardless of how long the mnemonic is, it should be the first thing written out on the exam.

Practice Multiple-Choice

Practice multiple-choice exams are perhaps the second-most effective tool of exam preparation. Practicing multiple-choice and seeing the same 100-150 multiple-choice questions two to three times throughout the semester is incredibly useful to train your brain of the patterns in multiple-choice.

Knowing why an answer is correct, and why others are incorrect is more valuable than getting a question correct. Also, practice rewriting the analysis of an issue from a multiple-choice answer.

Whiteboarding

Many students often overlook whiteboarding. Whiteboarding forces the student to prove what they know by actually writing it out. Often it is surprising how poorly you can write what you know! Whiteboarding allows the big picture to come into focus. Some choose not to whiteboard because they do not know where to begin when it comes to whiteboarding. It is beneficial for viewing topics in segments and illustrating the depth of essay questions.

To begin, choose an entire segment of the course, whiteboard it out, find what is missing from the topic, and then fill in those gaps. Putting those gaps of information on a whiteboard displays perceived knowledge to actual knowledge. So, whiteboard the entire subject to get a fuller understanding of the areas of knowledge you lack. Also, whiteboarding possible responses allows for targeting tested subjects. Thus, whiteboarding can be a helpful tool. After utilizing these exam tools, the next step is to exam prep "skeletons" for analysis.

Build a Skeleton

What is a skeleton? A skeleton is essentially the bones of the essay. It is the content of an outline or framework that should be memorized before the exam, like the mnemonic. For example, a skeleton is a general framework which encapsulates entire exam analyses. This is a pre-exam tool that is to be used intra-exam.

Creating Your Skeleton

So how do I create a skeleton? First, gather the solid number of a landmark or key cases that your professor repeated in class. Second, compile the cases or rules and form an outline using them. Essentially, the skeleton should address any and every potential issue that you may come upon in the exam. By having this prepared skeleton at the beginning of the essay, the substantive framework will be easy to fill in. Does it fit into an outline? The outline is different from the skeleton because the skeleton includes the substance that you write on the exam!

A sample outline might look like this:

1. Battery (elements)

   a. Intent to cause harmful/offensive contact

   b. Harmful/offensive contact occurred

   c. Absent consent

Whereas the sample skeleton would look like this:

1. (Battery) A battery occurs when one intends to cause a harmful or offensive contact of another, absent the consent of the person who was harmfully or offensively contacted.

2. (Intent) Intent exists when one has as their purpose the goal of bringing about a specific outcome.

3. (Harmful/offensive contact) A harmful or offensive contact exists when one makes contact with another in a manner that is perceived as harmful or offensive to the person being contacted.

4. (Absent consent) Absent of consent is displayed when the individual making the

claim did not portray that the individual consented to the actions of the other.

The above skeleton is a good distinction between what a skeleton should include as compared to an outline. The skeleton is the part that is memorized verbatim and is unchanging no matter the fact pattern. With a skeleton memorized, come exam day all you will have to do is fill in the fact pattern to the skeletons that you have already memorized.

Practice, Practice, Practice

Practice makes perfect, and practicing analysis drills is undoubtedly the way to making "A's" in law school. Practice drills like flashcards. Practice analysis segments. Practice writing essays. Do not go into the final exam without having taken practice exams. Lawyers do not go out and perform without having done a few practice sessions. Practice, practice, practice because (1) you must be able to issue spot, (2) answer multiple-choice questions, and (3) write a cogent essay. In the 1L year, issue spotting is huge. If you cannot spot the issues, you cannot get the points. Avoid writing in issues in the hopes that issue may exist. If the issue is a stretch, spot it, and move on, it is not likely that issue is a large part of the points. Identifying incorrect issues will waste your time and word count (if there is one). Issue spotting is simple. But there are many times after you begin to write that you may suddenly remember a potential issue from the fact pattern. If that occurs, take a breath and address it. Practicing spotting the issues early on will save you valuable time. Moreover, being able to spot all the issues during the first read will help you formulate the essay! In a class full of students able to spot all the issues, the better-formulated papers will get higher grades. So, if the essay has the substance and looks better, it will win out.

Hopefully, your professor has given the class a sample essay with a sample answer. This is a great way to identify spotting the correct issues at bar. If the professor has not provided any materials online or in the reserves, remember there are sites online. Look them up. They target law students with practice essays and practice answers. Read the essays and spot the issues. Also, see if the professor will let you submit a sample essay and answer for review, if so, writing out a sample answer and receiving feedback from the professor will greatly increase your readiness on exam day.

Remember, questions can only be formulated so many ways. The more you become familiar with how questions are phrased and how the issues are presented in a multiple-choice question, the better you will perform on exam day. When practicing multiple-choice questions, read the answers as to why one answer is right, and the other answers are wrong—even if you get the question right. This helps you hone in on the reasoning behind the right answers and explains why an answer that sounds correct is incorrect. When taking the exam, you will be pleasantly surprised at how familiar the questions will read.

By far, practicing essay writing is the most important practice you can do. Exams are primarily based on essays. You cannot afford to waste time about thinking what to write, even if you already know what to write. When you spot an issue, typing out the rule should be an instant reflex, you should not have to remind yourself what the rule is.

Assuming you wrote out the skeleton first, the first outline will be rough. In a timed environment, reasoning and substance fall by the wayside, if you have done essay writing practice, then it will be straightforward. Type out all the causes of actions and defenses you have learned. Knowing what to write is important. So, do not waste time hesitating on the known skeleton and outline. Read a practice essay and type it out. This is the best way to judge how prepared you are for the essay. After that, review your writing.

You must review your writing to ensure the basic theory of the case is correct. Then check to see if you have spotted all the issues. Next, check to see if the rules can be formulated better. Finally, ask yourself was this analysis an actual analysis that implemented "because" and "here." Many students make the mistake of stating the facts and fail to offer an excellent analysis. Do not be that student. Use the word "because" to bridge the facts and law.

The final exam is likely 80-100% of the overall grade. You must be "in it to win it." It would be foolish for you to think that you can show up and perform at your best without having done a single practice essay or practice multiple-choice questions. Therefore, practice essays, issue spotting, skeleton writing, and multiple-choice!

Drills

Practice drills are a terrific technique for acing exams because it trains your brains to remember your outline, skeletons, and mnemonics to be used on the exam. Several types of drills should be practiced. First, analysis drills should be practiced. It is imperative that the process of writing out analyses of each issue be drilled until they have been memorized verbatim. Where do you find the material to write out the analyses? By knowing your professor, from googling online, and from other law school resources! Mainly, find practice exams. It does not matter where they come from as long as they cover the issues you will be analyzing in your essay. When we wanted more practice exams, we found several on other law school's websites.

Teaching Others

Talk it out—questioning and talking out material with a partner also helps significantly with memorization. Get with a study group and ask each other questions. Ask each other to explain an issue, element, rule, or format. Then use memory devices from earlier in the book to remember important topics. These conversations will be stuck in your memory bank on test day.

Flashcards

For flashcards, there are two paths to encoding the information to regurgitate on the exam. The first is to manually enter the information, which means that you are taking the words of your professor and entering them into another medium verbatim. For example, the old-school drill of writing a sentence over-and-over again works when memorizing data and scripts. These types of drills are not tips that your professor is going to give you on how to succeed when taking their exam. The approach to take when considering your professor's state of mind is that they expect you to be professional and learn the material yourself. So, what should be on a flashcard? The cases and their corresponding rules. For example, *International Shoe* on one side of the flashcard; and on the other side: Minimum Contacts (topic) and "International Shoe created the legal rule for what has come to be known as minimum contacts within a state for specific jurisdiction. Thus, flashcards can be a helpful tool for memorizing parts of the issue and skeleton.

Multiple-Choice Drills

There is simply no way to overstate the importance of multiple-choice questions. Multiple-choice questions provide an array of issues that are helpful for your brain. In law school, multiple-choice is equivalent to pattern recognition in the LSAT, except in law school it applies to legal theory and procedure.

No question should ever look new. Even if the exam is all essay, do not decline to practice multiple-choice drills. They are a great way to improve your reasoning and understanding. The primary purpose of multiple-choice is not to get the answers right but to hone in on your reasoning.

If the exam is all essay, you can see the reasoning of the answer choices and use that as part of the analysis on the exam. The purpose is to examine the reasoning behind the choice. Read the answers, even the questions you got correct. Disregarding the reasoning of the questions you got correct is hazardous. Your reasoning may be incorrect or maybe a lucky guess, so hone in on the correct reasoning. Tailor your thinking to the correct answer. Questions about specific topics can only be presented in a limited amount of ways. Familiarize yourself with the manner in which tested topics are presented. This will significantly impact your multiple-choice performance. By becoming familiar with the questions and correct reasoning, you will be able to get through the multiple-choice portion without wasting valuable time.

Multiple-choice drills are not done just to improve multiple-choice skills, but analysis as well. The analysis portion of the correct and incorrect answers offer a plethora of valuable information. Read the rationales. Add them to overall knowledge and understanding of the topic. The analysis portion of an essay is the most heavily graded portion. Reading through the correct reasoning in a multiple-choice drill offers you valuable analytical skills. The rationale portion of the exam multiple-choice can provide a detailed analysis of the question or issue at bar. By doing multiple-choice drills, overall reasoning and knowledge of the subject will improve. Therefore, do multiple-choice, and do it often!

What If The Exam Is All Essay?

Even if an upcoming exam is purely essay, find multiple-choice questions on the subject and quiz yourself. Multiple-choice questions improve your reasoning and understanding because they force you to look at different rationales or theories you have which may be correct or incorrect. Once you have chosen the correct reasoning on issues, apply that reasoning to the essay in your analysis. Often, there is a full rationale for the answer provided in supplement books. They are terrific resources to plan out essays while using multiple-choice to answer the issue.

Prior To The Exam

First, have the supplies you need for the exam. Highlighters, pens, pencils, earplugs—whatever it takes for you to keep your thoughts organized while reading. Earplugs are a must have during the exam because many students begin typing madly as soon as the exam starts. Avoid distractions, minimize them. Before the exam, read the directions from the professor—the word count and the do's and don'ts. And finally, point distribution among essays. It would be very unfortunate to write a 2,000-word masterpiece when your professor only grades the first 1,000-words.

Essay Writing

As soon as the exam begins, write down the memorized skeleton or other material you might forget to include in your exam. Whatever the professor has hinted toward being tested upon, should be memorized. When reading an essay fact pattern, use a pencil to take note of issues and write out thoughts to include in the essay while reading. Read each sentence carefully. Flesh out each possible word for meaning, and remember to look first to the text!

Do not start typing or writing the essay before you have finished reading the entire fact pattern. The students that do this poorly forget critical information. You do not have to map out or outline your essay completely on scratch paper. Time is critical, so use your notes from your active reading and skeleton as a hybrid writing map.

Bolding, underlining, or *italicizing* as you type out the topics the professor is looking for stands out <u>VIVIDLY</u>. Remember, professors are grading over 100 papers at a time, and they do not catch every point a student includes in the paper. Ensure the professor sees the analysis by utilizing formatting and organization to your advantage. Look over time, points allotted, and the type of essay. Before submission, review your paper! In the mad dash under time constraints, it is easy to misspell a word. So, try to review before submission. Grammar is elementary. Therefore, do not forget to bold, underline, and italicize, so you stand out on exams.

Approaching the Exam

How one begins an exam is dependent upon the exam given. There are three types of exams in law school: (1) Closed book; (2) Open notes; and (3) Take-home exam.

Let us first discuss the most common, the closed book exam. A rule of thumb is to write down all of the issues and elements of the issues—remember the black letter law. The black letter law is the portion of the essay that sets forth the rules of issues which guide the analytical portion of your exam. Do not take a risk and make the mistake of forgetting black letter law when it is well within your scope of control. If you can get all the issues written out early, along with the rules that apply to them, then it will make for much better utilization of your time when you get to the analysis section. If there are both multiple-choice and essay, professors usually give a recommended allotment of time on each section or deliver those portions of the exam separately. If there is no allotment of time is recommended, then the approach taken is entirely a judgment call.

Here are some things to consider with a judgment call of the value of each section: (1) the approximate amount of time each section will take, and (2) the level of difficulty of each section. If you choose the multiple-choice first, then it is likely to refresh your memory on the upcoming material in the essay, but the reverse can be true, it can sometimes muck understanding of a topic. Alternatively, if the first choice is the essay, there may be less cloudiness as to whether certain elements are met due to limited exposure of incorrect answer choices on the multiple-choice. In the end, it boils down to whichever method you feel most comfortable.

The second type of exam is open notes and self-explanatory. Do not fall into the trap of having your outline or book(s) with you as a crutch. Study the subject more before the exam. Open note exams are very similar to a closed book exam. The open notes should be a reference to the framework because you will not have time to go through your outline or notes during the exam. Never use your book in scenario two (open notes) because it is much too dense. Have the key parts incorporated into a short outline. Only use the notes, outline, or book as a method of ensuring that the elements you need for a claim or defense are correct. Also, professors may require that all outside materials be turned in at the end of the exam.

The third type of exam is a take-home exam. Take-home exams typically have a time frame of which to complete them. The manner in which take-home exams are approached can vary. They are likely to be untimed or assigned for a several hour time period. Your take-home exam should be your best written and thought out the exam because of time to edit it.

To stand out on your take-home exams, be sure to do the following things: (1) Cite specific cases that used arguments that are necessary for your analysis; (2) Ensure that your paper is well-organized, is readable, and free from grammatical errors; And (3) reread the fact pattern diligently while looking for claims you may have missed.

Utilize all of the time you have for the exam. Do not turn it in early. Edit, then do more editing.

Housekeeping Matters

Know the environment in which you work best. If you do your best work in the library, work on the take-home exam there. Alternatively, if you work better at home, then work from there. Housekeeping matters concern your preference of where to work and how to work. Basically, as you approach the exam, choose your environment carefully.

Approaching Multiple-Choice Versus Essay

What approach is best to the multiple-choice versus essay dilemma? The multiple-choice versus essay dilemma is where the student can choose which section he or she will take first. Typically, when one section is over, the student cannot return to that section. Regardless what section is chosen, do not waste time dwelling on possible answer choices in the past, move on. If multiple-choice is your first pick, have scratch paper and pencil ready. When preparing to answer a question, always read the call of the question first. Like in the LSAT, multiple-choice questions have a call of the question at the end. The call is primarily an indicator to let the reader know which section of the law applies. Accurately read the call first, then approach the question itself. Be sure you discard irrelevant information that does not pertain to the call.

Again, read each line sentence by sentence. Breeze over the entire scenario in your first read, but take the time to encode the essential facts on the second read. After that, extract possible claims or defenses, then analyze. Often, professors include information that is not needed or relevant to get the student hung on a question. However, each sentence is also likely to provide some support or dissent from or to a claim. Therefore, know how to approach the essay and multiple-choice.

Actively Write

As you read the fact pattern, actively write down while outlining the information from the fact pattern to answer the essay question. As you read each line, make notes and review your outline to ensure it has the claims organized by element. Then, attach a fact to prove each element. Ensure that all claims are written, and if applicable or required, their defenses. Thus, actively write in your outline for the essay.

Create a Checklist

Create a checklist at the outset of the exam. The checklist should include: (1) all the main issues; (2) the elements to each of the spotted issues; (3) a brief synopsis as to what the arguments are for both sides; and (4) it should have an overarching theory of the case you are analyzing. Just as you may learn in a trial, the checklist is an effective way to ensure every issue is hit and analyzed or argued.

Approaching Multiple-choice

As with essay, always read the call of the question first. Reading the call of the question is an excellent way to keep you on track during your reading of the fact pattern. If a fact pattern has several questions, then it may be more beneficial to read the fact pattern first instead of trying to remember several individual calls-of-questions. Conversely, if there are only a few questions, it will not be difficult to read the call of the questions first, then go over the fact pattern.

Hide the Answers

Sometimes, there are multiple correct answers in multiple-choice questions. In such cases, the instructions will often ask you to choose the "most correct" one. A method that is efficient is to cover the answers with your hand or a sheet of paper, then answer the question without looking at the answer choices. By covering the answer, you force yourself to formulate your answer. After doing so, uncover the multiple-choice answers and match your answers with the closest option available. Also, remember to eliminate wrong answers, and skip difficult questions. Additionally, have a set amount of time which you will allow on a particular question. As a rule of thumb, if you do not know an answer, then skip it to save time and brain power. Go back and fill in that answer choice before the exam is up.

Analysis

This chapter of the book is dedicated to accurately analyzing a fact pattern using the applicable rules derived from case law. The analysis process you are about to read is unique because even the 2L who has only seen lackluster grades can get a grasp on the type of analysis that earns an "A." The analysis portion of the exam is the section with the majority of points. Use diligent preparation from the prior months in the semester on this section, apply the facts well, and you will earn top grades in your classes.

What Is The Analysis?

The analysis is the application of the fact pattern to the rules that evaluate arguments of an issue. There are several instructional books and chapters written on exam analysis, and for many classes, the professor will give an overview of what they are looking for in their exams. Avoid any uncertainty regarding the analysis segment of your essay by following the guide below.

How Should You Structure The Analysis?

The professor will probably tell you which format they expect the student to use in writing their exam essay. Professors prefer the IRAC or CREAC method because they want to see the conclusions drawn through constructing your analysis. It is a way to, in mathematical terms, proof your work. IRAC means Issue, Rule, Analysis, Conclusion. CREAC means Conclusion, Rule, Explanation, Application, Conclusion. They are the two most commonly used legal writing methods in law school.

IRAC is sometimes preferred over CREAC because professors want to see the conclusion through the construction of your analysis. However, this guide will show both analytical structures and utilize both IRAC and CREAC. Spot your issues and write your rules in an intelligible manner, then use one of the methods the moment you get to the analysis.

What Comes First In An Analysis?

How do you sculpt and organize the analysis an "A" essay demands? First, outline your analysis. Avoid omitting any information and use your time efficiently. Once you have spotted an issue and written the rule for it, jot down the exact words of the fact pattern that prove and depict the elements. Then, quote facts that prove the requirements for that particular rule. Place them in quotations as an indicator for the professor. Assuming you have read the fact pattern, highlight the portions of the essay that will lend support to your argument. Look at the fact pattern line-by-line, to avoid overlooking even the smallest detail.

Start Your Analysis

After you complete the essay outline, start typing. A crucial word that indicates the beginning of your analysis to professors is "<u>here</u>." It may seem repetitive to write this way, but it is what your professor expects. "Here" is an essential indicator for the construction of your argument. Next, insert the highlighted section of the fact pattern into the analysis. For the sake of redundancy, take for instance the conspiracy example once more. For example, you would write, "Here, A B and C may be charged with conspiracy if they agreed to rob the bank at an abandoned house, then took substantial steps to gather material in doing so." Remember, the professor has several essays to grade that all look very similar. So, make sure to increase the readability of your essay by adding indicator "here."

Sample Analysis

For example, let us say you spot the issue of conspiracy in your fact pattern. List the rule: "conspiracy is (1) when 2 or more persons (2) join together (3) to form an agreement to violate the law, and (4) then act on that agreement." Write out this rule the instant you spot the issue of conspiracy. Next, go through the fact pattern and highlight the exact words that prove the four elements of conspiracy listed above. The fact pattern states, "A B and C met up at an abandoned house and discussed plans to rob the bank. Additionally, they began gathering tools which could open a vault." Highlight this sentence and include it in your outline as a relevant factor that will lend support to your argument about conspiracy. Factors in law school are groups or individual pieces of evidence that lend credence to your case. Beside the highlighted mark of the fact pattern, you will write-out "conspiracy" so you know what this section applies to and do not have to spend mental legwork finding where it applies once you begin writing. Highlight and write down these facts immediately to not forget the issue. Time is a prevalent constraint when writing essays, so your time to edit is limited (more on this later in the "Time Management" chapter). In conclusion, outline issues and rules, highlight factors and watch your time when in the analysis or application section of an essay.

Distinguish Your Analysis

Distinguish your essay from the rest by underlining key phrases. Here, the important word to underline would probably be "conspire" since it is the issue and charge you want to initiate against A B and C. Underlining "conspire" in the analysis shows your professor an analysis as to why the conspirators would be charged. Continuing with the analysis construction, after you inject the facts verbatim from the fact pattern, actually begin analyzing those facts. For example, "Here, A B and C conspired to commit robbery because they met at an abandoned house and gathered tools which could break open a vault." Do not make conclusory statements without facts attached to your premise (e.g. "here A B and C are conspirators"), instead, tie the facts of your case (i.e., "vault tools" and "abandoned house") to your argument using the word "because." "Because" attaches the support your argument needs to be valid, so use it often, especially in your analysis section.

Analyze Both Sides

Analyze both sides of the arguments zealously. Give your audience, the professor, an indicator that the counter-argument is coming. This is achieved through using language such a "conversely" or "in contrast." Again, indicators here necessary to give a roadmap as to where the argument may go. They allow the reader to understand a change-up is coming, so they can prepare for different viewpoints.

Does Every Sentence Have Meaning?

Every sentence in a fact pattern does not necessarily add to the claim. However, when going through the fact pattern, assume that it does. Professors carefully craft exams. They give points for each issue or counter issue raised. Thus, to get exceptional grades, think about checking off each issue and counter issue in your head to keep track of about how many points you have. The remaining portion of the point distribution is from the rules, framing of issues, and organization. Look at every sentence and see if you can derive a point from that sentence by merely using it as the support for the arguments or counters that you are building. Typing several thousand words into a short exam does not automatically translate to the idea that you know an issue. So, remember to concisely show off your legal analysis using cogent language that derives points from most sentences.

To make an "A," explain your work more articulately than others in your class while hitting the issues within each sentence. Spot the significant issues, talk about them in detail to show the professor that you spotted those issues, then receive points for finding them. For example, back to the original hypothetical where we have A B and C partake in a conspiracy. What would be another point to capture in the conspiracy hypothetical? The fact that A B and C met at the abandoned house and began gathering tools. This indicates a sub-issue in the claim of conspiracy, a "substantial step" toward actually committing the robbery. Forming your analysis this way in the exam is the most beneficial because it is likely what the professor expects.

Here, the support of the argument comes from merging the fact pattern with the law to conclude the sub-issue. Thus, the student can gain points for the sub-issue by tying the fact pattern into it for support. Conclusively, the bulk of the points can be derived from this section. We have reviewed how to analyze an issue accurately; structure the analysis; show meaning; derive points from every sentence; and finally, how to discuss sub-issues to get maximum point.

Because

The analysis portion of the essay, the most important word to use is "because." "Because" links facts and legal theory together. Whether you write in IRAC or CREAC, the bulk of the points awarded on any law school essay comes from the analysis section because it is where the knowledge of the material is from the semester is illustrated by the student.

Students often fail at putting together a thoughtful analysis because they presume that somehow professors know what they are expressing, but this is not the case. Instead, articulate a coherent analysis that uses "because" to tie facts with legalese. Make the sentences simple.

Conclusory Statements Instead Of Using "Because"

So where do most students go wrong in an essay? Typically, students make conclusory statements inside the essay argument instead of analyzing whether their conclusion is correct. Conclusory statements are conclusions arrived upon without analysis. For example, using the hypothetical conspiracy from the "Analysis" chapter a student might conclude that, "A, B, and C committed conspiracy." This is a conclusory statement because it has no analysis attached to it. It does not illustrate how or why A, B and C committed conspiracy, but it proclaims that they did commit conspiracy nonetheless.

Again, the better approach is to use the word analytical word "because" and join the fact pattern and the crime together. In other cases, use the word "because" to join the elements and the crime together. For example, better use of a fact pattern with the crime of conspiracy inside it might be: "A, B, and C committed the crime of conspiracy <u>because</u> they agreed and met at an abandoned location and took the substantial steps of furthering the crime." This sentence is much more useful to the professor to determine how you arrived at such a conclusion. By including the word "because," the sentence has now been transformed from a conclusory one to an analytical one.

In conclusion, remember that both sides stipulate facts before a fact pattern is formed. In other words, the fact pattern contains facts agreed upon by both parties as to the events which occurred. Your job as a student is to join fact and the law by using the word "because" to illustrate your analytical skill as a future lawyer. Therefore, constantly use the word "because" to show the professor your analytical skills.

Exam Taking

The day before the exam, study the material, practice multiple-choice and essay writing. Practice writing down solid rule statements. Know the elements of claims because they are imperative in proving your case. The day of the exam, wake up early, eat a healthy breakfast, and give yourself plenty of time to get prepared. Arrive early, do not be late for the exam.

Exams can be incredibly stressful. So, locate the exam room, claim your seat early, get comfortable, and prepare your laptop. Think over last-minute issues before the exam, begin with a clear mind. Other classmates will be conversing about their last exams, expectations, future exams, or what they will do after the exam. Ignore them. You need to soak in as much information as you can before the exam. Have confidence in yourself.

During The Exam

Whether short answer or long answer essay, it is always best to outline the answer first. Although you may be tempted to put words on your screen, do not start writing right away. Briefly outline the essay answer you intend to write. Your essay answer will be more focused, and the professor will see this. Going directly into an essay question is a sure way to miss topics and under-analyze portions of the law.

As stated before, have a format that is easy to follow. If the professor has not given any guidance on how he or she likes answers formatted, then refer back to IRAC. A broad issue statement is necessary to catch all the claims each party can bring. Identify all the issues in one issue statement. Save yourself valuable time by pointing out all the issues at once. After you have identified the issues, separate portions should be construed for each issue, discuss the possible claims. Then insert the rules you have memorized from the skeleton.

Next, the analysis portion is likely what you professor cares for the most. When forming your analysis, it is critical to remember that statements are of analysis and not of conclusions. To ensure that your statement is an analysis statement, remember, use words such as "because" and "therefore." By using those indicator words, the statement becomes one of analysis. Conclusions do not have to be lengthy. In fact, typically they are usually very short and generally consist of no more than, "A is likely to succeed on a claim of "x" against B because A can successfully demonstrate elements 1, 2, and 3" or "A is unlikely to succeed on a claim of "y" because A may not be able to demonstrate element 3 of claim "y."

Read the Call of the Question First

Before you read the fact pattern, read the call of the question. This way you know what to look for in the fact pattern. By doing this, you will be able to focus your reading on those specific issues. If the professor allows you to have an outline, review your notes or outline after spotting issues in the fact pattern and write down the appropriate claims, defenses, and exceptions that exist. Ensure that you have pulled all the pertinent information from the fact pattern to your notes and outline. Quickly, order your notes and outline in the manner that you believe is best for the exam.

Organizing can be as simple as drawing a line between specific segments or numbering each segment. As you write, cross-out each segment that you have completed, ensuring that you do not miss anything. If you think of any other issues or claims while writing, fill those into the appropriate place as you go. The goal is to provide yourself with a concise writing guide to an essay. You will not waste time going back and forth reading and re-reading if you do this step correctly, you will have a guide that will effectively keep you on track and move through the exam.

Unless the exam question asks the student explicitly to consider outside facts or possibilities, do not waste time arguing issues that are not included in the fact pattern. There are no points to gain from doing this, and the clock is ticking. Be direct when writing your answers, there is no time to go back and re-write issues. You get one go-at-it, so do not waste time needlessly writing, know what issue to address, and address it appropriately. Blindly typing anything hoping to pick up points is a massive waste of time and rarely productive.

Be direct and concise, follow your outline, and complete your essay. Arguing extraneous issues is not only a waste of time, but some professors will also mark students off for this. Approach time management very seriously when writing your essay, because knowing the material is useless if you run out of time to discuss it.

Answering Multiple-Choice Questions

There are several approaches to tackling multiple-choice questions. What works best for the authors is reading the "call of the question" first. If you read the call of the question first, you are privy as to pertinent material. This allows you to read the question once and then pick out the best answer. By already knowing what to look for when you start reading the fact pattern, you will potentially save time by not having to read the fact pattern a second time. Do not pick out the first right answer that you see.

Multiple-choice exams require you to pick out the best answer, and there may be two or three answers that could be correct. Instead of picking out the first answer choice that could be right, eliminate the answer choices you know are incorrect or less right and then make your selection from there. Choose your answer and stick with it. Do not waste time thinking about the other possible answers and do not go back to change your answers. Skip answers if needed. If you do not have the answer right away, eliminate wrong factors and move on, do not get hung up on one question. Then, go back and choose answers for questions that you have skipped. By going through the entire multiple-choice section, you may recall the information necessary to help you with other questions.

By starting the essay first, you can get the written portion out of the way. Essay questions are normally worth more than the multiple-choice portions, so spend extra time on what can garner you the points. Conversely, by starting the multiple-choice first, the testing material can aid you before considering the essay. It is essential to know how much time you want to devote to the essay since the essay is likely to be the most valuable part of the exam. Having a multiple-choice cut-off time is necessary. If you do not finish the multiple-choice in the time allotted, remember what questions that were neglected and set up an appropriate amount of time to return to those questions near the end of the exam. If you do anything to the multiple-choice answers after finishing, then ensure the answers are bubbled in properly. Lastly, review your essay for spelling or grammar mistakes.

Underlining, Bolding, and Italicizing

One highly underrated technique to making good grades in law school is changing the ***font of your rules to jump off the page at the professors***. The professor wants to know you understand what you are writing about and that you know the law. Additionally, professors grade on average up to 100 students per class, which means they have to look over the same essays, time after time. One good way to stand out in your essay, especially if you are very prepared and know all of your definitions, is by **bolding** or *italicizing* your rules. By doing this simple technique, the professor will be thankful that you wrote in a nice, orderly, and concise manner. They can also easily spot where you have illustrated your knowledge of the issues. In addition, if you have used formatting to illustrate important points in your writing, it is less likely the professor might accidentally overlook these crucial points. Thus, every point you include will be more likely spotted in your essay. Formatting is an easy trick to ensure readability for the professor!

Time Management

Exams are timed, and in most instances, the time allocated is nowhere near the amount of time that would be necessary to write and perfect an ideal essay. Due to the time crunch, it can be difficult to spot every single issue, exceptions to the issues, and the possible outcomes to each issue. However, with adequate time management, you can set yourself up for success.

Manage Your Time Effectively

Time management requires that you manage your time both effectively and productively. Time management is not wasting time planning out how much time you are going to devote to each issue you have spotted. Successful exam takers take note of the issues spotted and allocate the appropriate amount of time for each portion. Speed is essential;

however, speed without practice and experience may be detrimental to your grade. As mentioned in the previous section, "Practice, Practice, Practice," the speed needed to complete the exam in time will come naturally with the practice you undergo during test preparation.

Training is essential because come exam day you will not want to waste one-second thinking of what to type out for a particular answer, you will spot the issue, apply the facts in the analysis, and type the answer. If you practice writing answers to sample questions before the exams, you know what phrases will work in an exam, you will not waste valuable time thinking about how to transition from one topic to another, and you will already have mastered this skill.

Have The Material Memorized

Knowing how to "IRAC" quickly and efficiently is vital in exam writing. Ideally, the only thing you should have to worry about on an exam is spotting the issues and applying the facts. If you have your class material memorized and know how to write that material into an IRAC form that you have memorized, the only thing you are battling on test day is the clock. As you spot an issue, lay out the elements of the issues and their rules immediately.

There are two essential methods for being able to recall issues quickly. One approach, useful for closed book examinations, in which memorization is vital, is for students to jot down all crucial claims or elements that they believe are likely to be on the exam before even reading the fact pattern. By doing this, students practically mind-dump everything that they have memorized to reveal what may have been forgotten and what they should try to remember as they read through the fact pattern. As beneficial as this approach is, this approach could be a humongous waste of time if the issue is not actually on the exam. Some professors tell their students to follow this method, and it is beneficial if the professor allows time for this on the test.

Make Your Essay Flow

Another approach is to read through the fact pattern and write out the full issues, elements, and rules. Students that take this approach are in an excellent position to organize the material and flow of the essay before one begins to write. Overall, you must choose the method that is best for you. Our recommended approach, however, is to read through the fact pattern slowly and write down the issues as you spot them.

After the Exam

After the exam, you may be tempted to dwell over the issues you spotted in the essay. This is pointless. The exam is over, and there is absolutely nothing you can do to change your answers. Worrying about where you potentially went wrong will only hinder you as you study for your next final. Once you have recuperated, move on to studying for your next exam.

Transferring

Transferring is a topic that few students openly discuss. It is not a topic in which you will find helpful guidance online. And it is not a topic that your law school's administration would be happy to assist you in. There are several reasons why a law student would want to transfer schools. Some students want to move closer to a specific locale, some students may be intrigued by a particular program that another law school offers, and some seek to transfer to a higher ranked school. Whatever your reason for transferring is, it does not matter. This chapter aims to guide you through the pros and cons of transferring, how to go about transferring, and what to do after you transfer.

Visiting Semester

Before we dive into our discussion about transferring, let us talk about the visiting year or visiting semester. A visiting year or visiting semester allows the law student to complete credit at a different law school while remaining a student at the previous law school. For example, students who want to take part in a study abroad program that is not offered by their school may "visit" another school for a summer semester to do so. There are also many students who want to practice law in a particular region or city; these students may spend a visiting year or visiting semester at a local law school to build a professional network in that area. There are numerous other reasons as to why a student may want to "visit" another law school, but the two reasons mentioned above are the most common.

Students who complete a visiting year or visiting semester must be cautious as to how many credit hours will be received and how many of those are transferrable. Many law schools require that the student complete a minimum of sixty credit hours from that law school to graduate. Even though a student may have earned more than ninety credit hours from two different schools, that student needs to be cognizant of how many credit hours were earned from that student's law school. Most simply put, whichever school that you accumulate 60 or more credit hours will be the school in which the degree is awarded.

Pros And Cons Of Transferring

List the pros and cons of transferring law schools. If you are thinking of transferring, whatever reason you have for transferring is likely to be the main reason on your pro side of your transfer pros-and-cons list. Mostly, transferees look for one or two of the three reasons listed: (1) better-ranked school; (2) location; or (3) cheaper tuition. All of these are valid pros and outweigh any number of drawbacks you can imagine. We will not spend any more time telling you about your reasons for transferring, but there are specific cons to be cognizant of before you decide to transfer.

One author of this book transferred to a different law school for all of the three reasons mentioned above. After about two weeks into the transfer school, this author realized the number of cons very quickly that transferring can have. If you have never had the "new-kid" experience before, get ready to experience it. During the 1L year, students are generally split up into different sections with each section having the same schedule, because of this, bonds are quickly formed within each 1L section, and several cliques emerge. Although the second year is not divided up into sections, the cliques remain, and as a transfer student, you are likely to be on the outside looking in. There are a few easy ways to combat the "new-kid" syndrome. Be outgoing, get involved in student events, talk to whoever sits next to you in class and see what happens.

Another possible con is the cost of the new law school. Many law schools offer their initial students scholarships; however, when you transfer it is not likely that you will receive any scholarship money. You will likely pay the full sticker price for tuition when you transfer. If, after, considering all of the cons and you still want to transfer you will need to know the best methods for going about your transfer. Attending any law school with the goal of transferring after your first year may be a good motivator for achieving top grades, but in reality, the beginning of your first year is way too early to be thinking of transferring. Serious considerations for transferring needs to be done around the middle of your second semester. By this time, you will have a good idea of what you can expect grade-wise, and you can make your considerations from there. Remember, the golden rule of transferring is: do not talk about transferring. Revealing a desire to transfer to other students may isolate you from groups you need to be successful.

Forming a "transfer students clique" can be helpful, but there are apparent caveats as to why you may want to avoid doing that. The most beneficial method for transfer students wanting to integrate with the student body is to join an organization on campus. Joining an on-campus organization puts the transfer student into a group of like-minded individuals and the new-kid syndrome will start to vanish from there.

What Credits Transfer

Before you spend any money sending in transfer applications, take note of how many of your accumulated credits will transfer. For instance, a law school that requires four hours of Torts may not accept the five or six credit hours of Torts that you received from your previous law school. Also, some law schools may put restrictions on what classes are transferable and what classes are not. Most law schools allow students to transfer up to thirty hours from an ABA-accredited law school. If you have taken summer semester classes at your first law school, these credits may count for nothing.

Class Rankings

Class rankings and GPA's reset at the transfer law school. Many transfer students do just as well at their new higher ranked schools; however, higher ranked schools tend to attract higher caliber students, so be mindful of this. If you have done well at your first law school, you may have been able to grade-on to several different journals and even law review. You may also have done well in your moot court competitions and invited to join one of the school's teams. When you transfer, any grade-on or invitation that you received will mean nothing at a new school. You may have to prove yourself all over again just to be given the same recognition you have already achieved.

Acquiring Necessary Documents

Many transfer applications require at least one letter of recommendation from one of your 1L professors. Therefore, it is wise to build a good rapport with at least two of your 1L professors to ensure that you can obtain at least one letter of recommendation for your transfer application. Once you begin looking at law schools to transfer into, pay particular attention to what each school requires for transfer applications. Obtaining final grades is a demanding process. It was a tiresome experience. Hopefully, your current school will not delay when it comes to students who seek to transfer. Therefore, think about the above-mentioned considerations before transferring!

Conclusion

In conclusion, we hope you enjoyed this book! The authors carefully crafted each chapter of this book. We have included what we, as law students, have found to be the most useful throughout our law school careers. The aforementioned chapters convey, in the most concise way possible, general techniques that the authors have found to lead to success.

Each method that we have discussed is not unique to us. Every year, thousands of law students across the world employ the very methods that we have compiled for you. These methods are used because they are effective, they are tried and true, and they have helped us achieve success in law school.

We hope that you find this book helpful and that you too achieve the success you desire in law school.

About the Authors

Nathaniel Le graduated with a B.A. in History from the University of Texas, Arlington. Following college, Nathaniel enlisted in the United States Marine Corps. He was recognized for his actions in Afghanistan. Before deciding to pursue a career in law, Nathaniel worked professionally in the telecommunications industry. Nathaniel has served as the President of the Asian Pacific American Law Student Association at Barry University and is the Vice-Justice for Phi Alpha Delta's Harlan Chapter. He is currently a 3L at the University of Oklahoma College of Law.

Brandon Salter graduated cum laude with a B.A. in Law and Criminology from the University of Florida. He is one of only three 1L's awarded the Dean's Full Scholarship Award, which is Barry Law's highest scholarship. He is currently a 3L at Barry University Dwayne O. Andreas School of Law. His academic excellence has continued into law school and beyond, as he is currently a legal intern at a prominent mass tort firm in Orlando. In addition to academia, Brandon is a Single Engine Land pilot and member of the Federal Aviation Administration.

Kali Stauss graduated with a B.A. in English from the University of Florida. She is currently a 3L at Barry University Dwayne O. Andreas School of Law. She is a graduate from the University of Florida, Miss Gainesville USA 2012, former public-school educator, and certified athletic coach. Kali is heavily involved in community service, a member of the Junior League of Greater Orlando, and a member of the Coastal Conservation Association of Florida. She is an avid outdoorsman, angler, diver, and loves taking advantage of the Florida Sunshine at any chance possible.

Made in the USA
Middletown, DE
02 November 2020